Cassowary Coast - Count on Country

Written by
Pamela Galeano

Illustrated by
Dorothy Webster (Mirrimum)

Cassowary Coast - Count on Country

First published 2010

National Library of Australia Cataloguing -in- Publication entry.

Author:	Galeano, Pamela Agnes, 1943-
Title:	Cassowary Coast count on country / Pamela Galeano ; illustrator, Dorothy Webster.
Edition:	1st ed.
ISBN:	9780980494723 (pbk.)
Target Audience:	For pre-school age.
Subjects:	Counting--Juvenile literature.
	Australian languages --Juvenile literature.
Other Authors/Contributors:	
	Dorothy Webster
Dewey Number:	513.211

Illustrations by Dorothy Webster , rendered in acrylic on paper

Prepress & layout by Daryl Dickson Wildcard Art

Text of this book in Arial

Printed by Boolarong Press

Author's Dedication

In memory of Hazel Alpin of Mona Mona Mission

Illustrator's Dedication

For my Grandparents, Thomas Barclay-Miller and Grandma Nora

We wish to thank Jirrbal Elder Uncle Ernie Grant for sharing his tribal language.

one 1

One large cassowary walking on the beach,

yunggul 1

Yunggul large gunduy walking on the beach,

two 2

two lucky herons flying out of reach,

bulayi 2

bulayi lucky majala flying out of reach,

three 3

three dingo pups playing with their toys,

balan 3

balan ganabirra pups playing with their toys,

four 4

four black cockatoos making lots of noise,

bulayi-bulayi 4

bulayi-bulayi gidila making lots of noise,

five 5

five big barra swimming out to sea,

yungal bulayi-bulayi 5

yungal bulayi-bulayi big yugurr swimming out to sea,

six 6

six Ulysses butterflies in a corkwood tree,

garburrun garburru 6

garburrun garburru Ulysses gugunburr in a corkwood tree,

seven 7

seven python snakes hatching up a gum,

bulan bulayi-bulayi 7

bulan bulayi-bulayi maguy hatching up a gum,

eight 8

eight little crocodiles learning from their mum,

balan yungal bulayi-bulayi 8

balan yungal bulayi-bulayi little gugagay learning from their mum,

nine 9

nine hungry pelicans swimming near the shore,

balan garburrun-garburru 9

balan garburrun-garburru hungry ngugurrbal swimming near the shore,

ten 10

ten biting green ants - I don’t want any more!

yunggul bulayi balan bulayi-bulayi 10

yunggul bulayi balan bulayi-bulayi biting ngulbuny - I don’t want any more!